Elizabeth A. Hogan

how to pray with ICONS

An Introduction

NOVALIS Gracewing.

© Novalis, Saint Paul University, Ottawa, Canada, 1998.
First published by Novalis as *Praying with Icons: An Introduction for Children* in 1988.

Cover: Icon of the Nativity of Our Lord Jesus Christ, from the Church of Saint Sophia in Rome.
Editor: Chris Humphrey
Layout and cover design: Gilles Lépine

The icons in this booklet are from the
Ukrainian Catholic Church of Saint Sophia, Rome, Italy.

Biblical quotations are from
The New American Bible and the *Revised Standard Version*.

Novalis
49 Front St. East, Second Floor
Toronto, Ontario, Canada
M5E 1B3
1-800-387-7164 or (416) 363-3303

Gracewing, Fowler Wright Books
2 Southern Avenue
Leominster, Herefordshire HR6 0QF
England

British Library Cataloguing-in-Publication Data
A record for this book is available from the British Library.
ISBN: 085244-459-1

Canadian Cataloguing-in-Publication Data
Tataryn, M. (Myroslaw), 1956–
 How to pray with icons: an introduction

Rev. 2nd ed.
 Includes 12 removeable stick-on reproductions of icons, from the (Ukrainian Catholic) Church of Saint Sophia, Rome, Italy
ISBN 2-89088-348-5

 1. Icons–Cult—Juvenile literature. 2. Catholic Church—Prayer-books and devotions—English—Juvenile literature. I. Title.

BV212.T38 1997   j246'.53   C97-900604-X

*To those who are for me
Christ's sign of his abiding love:
Marusia, Myroslawa and Anastasia*

*A thank you to Marusia, my wife
who helped edit and proof the text.*

Contents

Preface 5
The Transfiguration of Christ 8
The Nativity of the Most Holy Mother of God 10
The Annunciation 12
The Nativity of Our Lord 14
The Theophany of Our Lord 16
Meeting Our Lord in the Temple 18
The Entry into Jerusalem 20
The Crucifixion of Our Lord 22
The Resurrection of Our Lord 24
The Ascension of Our Lord 26
The Descent of the Holy Spirit 28
The Dormition of the Mother of God 30
Suggestions for Parents and Teachers 32

Preface

Welcome! I greet you as we begin How to Pray with Icons; *I greet you as we begin our journey. Icons are special paintings which bring us closer to Christ, his Most Holy Mother and the saints. Icons have been called windows onto Heaven, and to pray with icons is to journey through this window – into Heaven.*

Such a journey requires that we prepare ourselves mentally, physically and spiritually. To pray with icons we need to be comfortable, quiet and attentive to what we are doing. That's the first step.

The second step is to check our maps and prepare our provisions. We must recognize the path we want to follow and be sure that we have everything we need. So, remove the numbered pictures of the icons from the middle of the book and prepare to moisten their backs and paste them in on the appropriate page of the book. But finish reading the rest of this introduction first, since it will help you to understand what you are seeing.

Icons are beautiful because we can see through them to Heaven. But icons can also be very strange if we don't understand the "signs" within them that guide us on our journey through the window into Heaven.

Icons are not photographs; they are paintings that invite us to meet Christ through events that really happened and people who really lived. At the same time, however, icons are not "realistic" paintings; rather, they are symbols which reveal, in an artistic manner, a profound spiritual truth – the mysterious reality of God's presence in human life. That's why icons always feature real people.

In an icon the central figure – usually Christ, the Mother of God or a saint – is always the largest. Other people in the icon are physically smaller. In this way the painter, or iconographer, tells us that these people, even though they have a role to play in our faith journey, are less important than the central figure.

The background of icons is gold, a colour which symbolizes the glory of Heaven. We also note that icons contain no shadows. That's because Heaven's light shines evenly on the holy people and other elements of creation depicted in the icon, revealing their truth and beauty. We seldom find dark areas either. If they exist, as in the icon of the Nativity, Christ is shown as if going into the darkness of the cave, for it is he who brings light into the darkest corners of the world.

Colours are very significant. White and gold are Christ's colours. This is especially evident in icons portraying him as a young child. When portrayed as an adult, Christ often wears a red inner robe covered with a blue cloak. Red is a sign of Christ's divinity, while blue is a sign of his humanity. He is God (red) but he takes on the human (blue/green). On the other hand, the colours for the Mother of God's clothing are reversed: her inner robe is blue (human) but covered with a cloak of red (divine). She is a human who became "divinized" (the first saint).

Finally, I want to stress again that icons draw our attention to the centre. That's because the central figure is where we meet Christ. Only later do we see the rest of the icon and begin to contemplate those things and people which surround our meeting with him. Christ leads us on our journey: through him and with him we make our way to Heaven. The others, the saints, are there as our companions – our friends who help us along the path. They show us that we never travel alone!

We begin our journey by climbing a mountain . . . .

The Transfiguration of Christ

"Peter said to Jesus: 'Master, how good it is for us to be here'" (Luke 9:33).

These are the words of the apostle Peter as he sees his teacher Jesus transformed in glory on Mt. Tabor. Peter, John and James (in the lower portion of the icon) follow their Master up the mountain to be with him while he prays. While praying, Jesus is transfigured, and two Old Testament figures appear: Moses (to his left) and Elijah (to his right). The apostles then hear God's voice say: "This is my Son, my Chosen One. Listen to him" (Luke 9:35).

To begin praying with icons we start with the one which an iconographer first paints: the Transfiguration. It teaches us the attitude which we must have if we are to be with Jesus, if we are to pray. We must settle down, relax and feel "how good it is for us to be here."

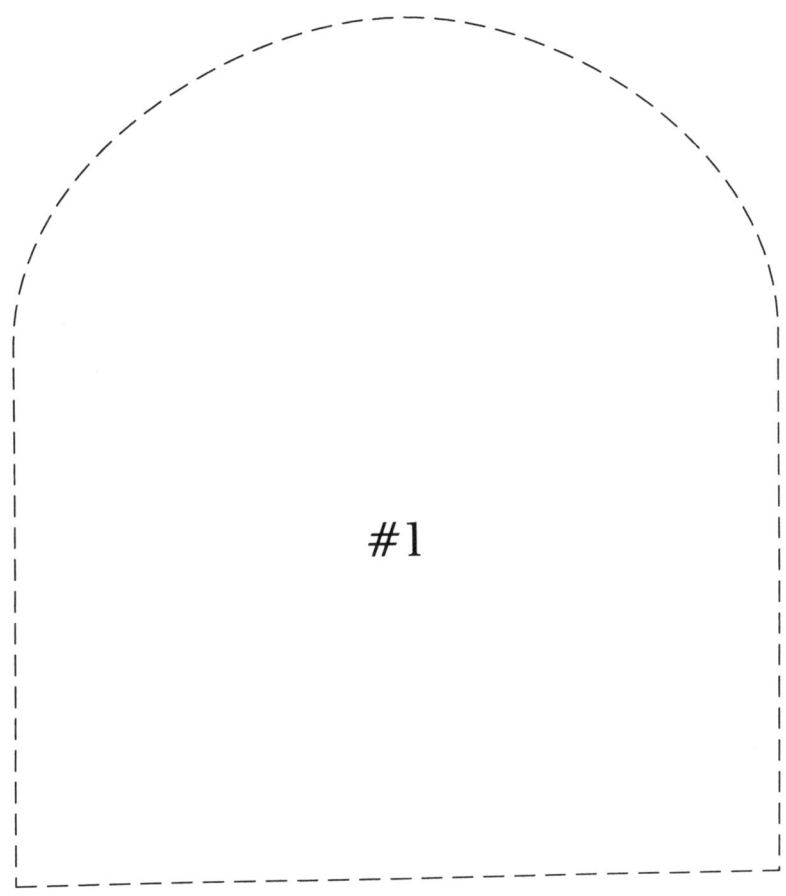

#1

Icon of the Transfiguration of Christ

Tropar – *You were transformed, O Christ our God, showing your glory to your disciples as much as they could understand. At the intercessions of the Mother of God make your everlasting light shine upon us sinners. O Giver of Light, glory to you.*

The Nativity of the Most Holy Mother of God

The first major feast day of the liturgical year is the Nativity of the Mother of God. Anna (the central figure lying on the bed) and Joachim have a daughter whom they name Mary. The child Mary (being washed in the basin) is a sign of God's promise to be with us. Mary is a sign of God's promise of salvation.

Anna is the central figure because she is the agent through whom God works. We know from the story of Anna and Joachim that they are very old and unable to have children. But God works a miracle. And so it is in our lives: we may not feel good, we may not feel holy, but God can work miracles in and through us. We can become good, we can become holy, we can bring new life into the world.

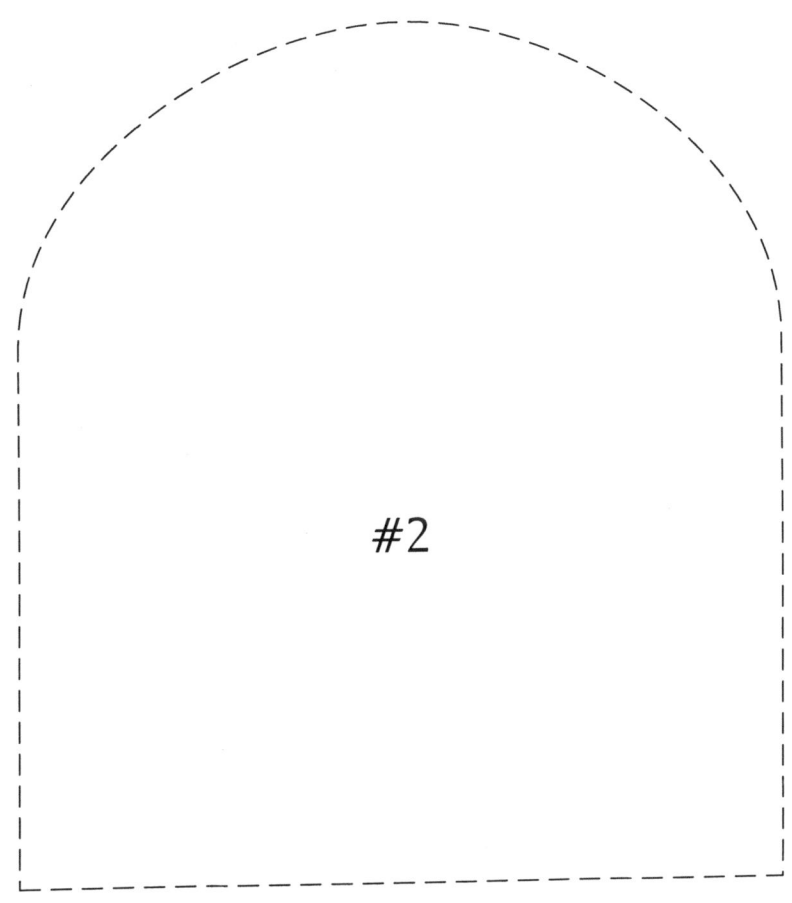

Icon of the Nativity of the Mother of God

Tropar – *Your birth, O Mother of God, has brought joy to the entire world: for from you has shone the Sun of Righteousness, Christ our God. He has released us from the curse and blessed us; he has made death have no effect, and given us eternal life.*

The Annunciation

New life is not brought into the world by our efforts alone – we are partners in the new creation. The Annunciation is the beginning of new creation. Gabriel brings God's promise of a Saviour, but the promise can only become real with Mary's "Let it be done to me as you say."

In prayer we must not fear; rather, we must allow Christ to speak to us and the Holy Spirit to dwell in us. Note that Mary is standing. She is attentive, she is open, yet she does nothing but accept Gabriel's words. Gabriel does all the action: he comes, he speaks and he leaves. But Mary is the blessed one, Mary is the holy one, Mary is the God-bearer. We must wait, we must hear God speak, we must co-operate with the Lord and become God-bearers.

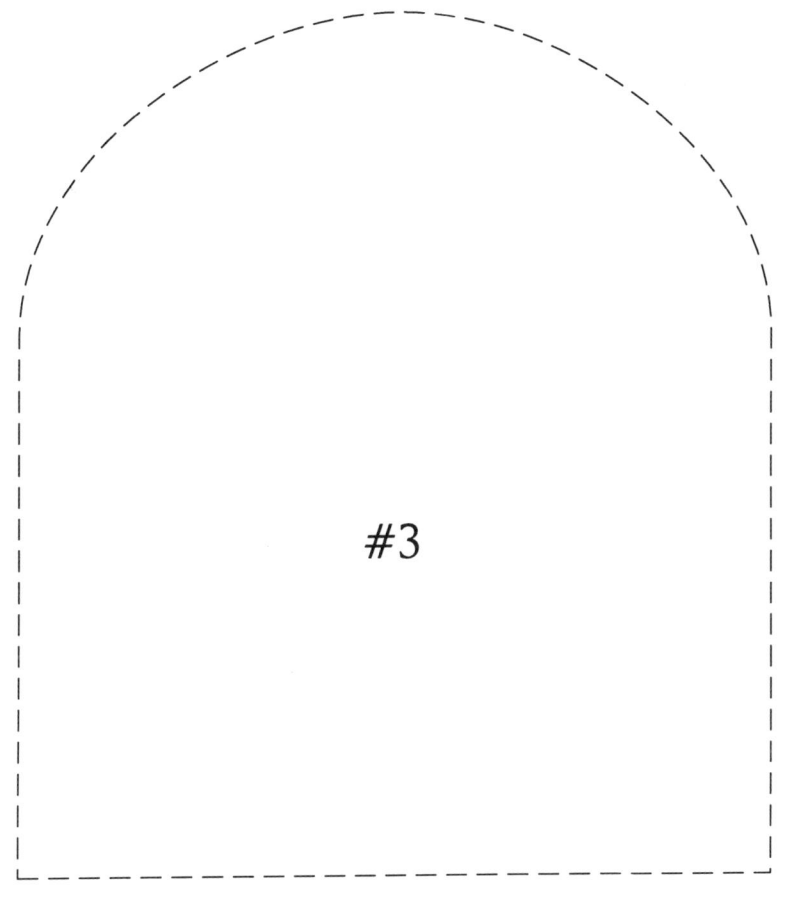

Icon of the Annunciation

Tropar – *Today is the crown of our salvation and the manifestation of the mystery that is from all eternity. The Son of God becomes the Son of the Virgin, and Gabriel announces the good tidings of grace. Therefore let us also join him and cry aloud to the Mother of God: "Hail, you who are full of grace, the Lord is with you."*

The Nativity of Our Lord

"The Word became flesh and dwelt among us" (John 1:14).

Mary brings the Son into the world. God becomes a human being: Jesus of Nazareth. Humanity is the dwelling place of God. The world is the resting place for the Son of God. The animals share their home with Christ. But that home, the cave, is also the place where he will be laid after his Crucifixion. That is why he is wrapped as if for burial, lying upon a coffin.

People react in various ways to the birth of Christ. Mary turns away, foreseeing the sorrow that will come. Joseph (in the left-hand corner) worries, not knowing what to believe. The midwives (on the right) wash him, just as they would wash any other newborn child. The shepherds stand and stare in amazement. How do we react to Christ's coming? Do we share his mother's pain? Do we doubt with Joseph? Are we unmoved like the midwives? Are we awed like the shepherds? Or like the animals do we open our hearts – the homes of our inner selves – and welcome the birth of the Lord?

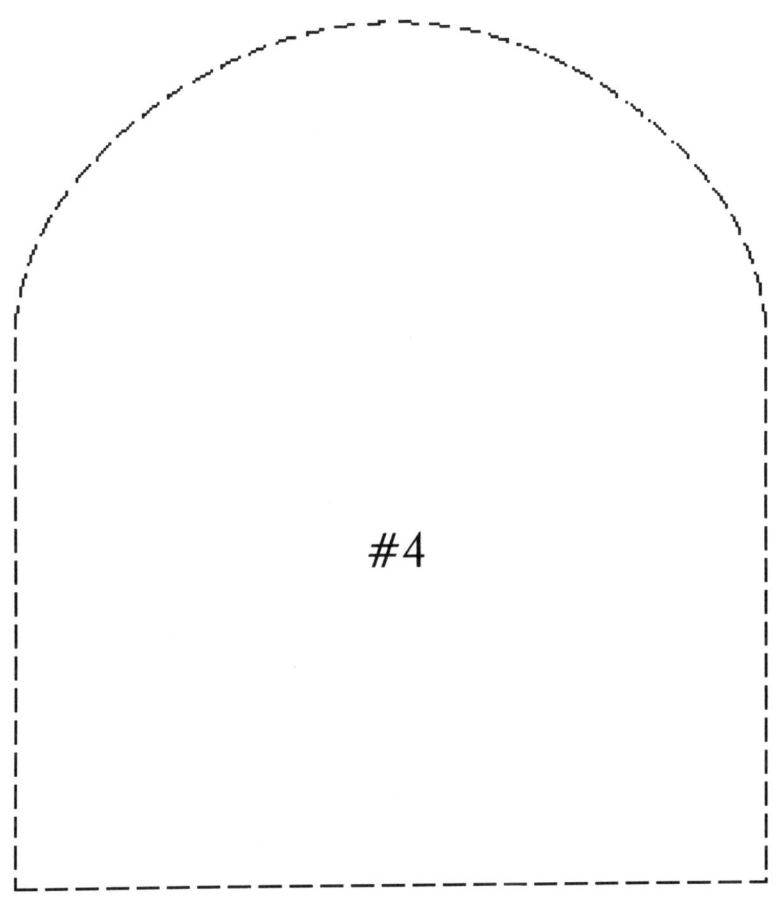

Icon of the Nativity of Our Lord Jesus Christ

Tropar – *Your Nativity, O Christ our God, has shone upon the world with the light of knowledge: for they who adored the stars, through the stars were taught to worship you, the Sun of Righteousness, and to know you as the Orient from on high. O Lord, glory to you.*

The Theophany of Our Lord

At the feast of the Theophany, we not only celebrate Christ's baptism, but also the first revelation of the Father, Son and Holy Spirit – the Holy Trinity. In the Theophany, which means "manifestation of God" or "revelation of God," we discover that, through Jesus, we can come to know the Holy Spirit who dwells over the Son, and the Father who declares Jesus as the Son.

This mystery is beyond comprehension. The little man in the water is a symbol for the Jordan River which flows backwards, because it is so amazed that God could become human. Water no longer brings death – by entering and immersing himself in it, Jesus, the Son of God, transforms the water into a source of life. Through baptism we all enter into an awareness of this great mystery that God is three, and yet one. Through baptism we die to our old selves and are born into Christ. To continue our journey we must renew our baptismal promise to die and rise with Christ.

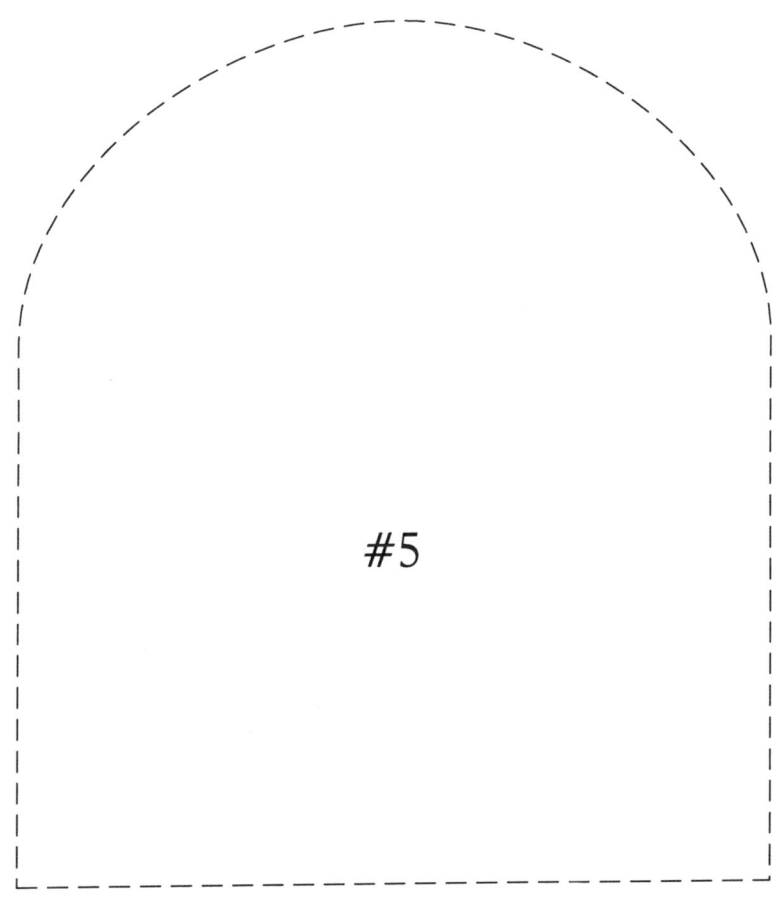

Icon of the Theophany of Our Lord

Tropar – *When you, O Lord, were baptized in the Jordan, the worship of the Trinity was made manifest. For the voice of the Father bore witness to you, calling you the beloved Son, and the Spirit in the form of a dove confirmed his Word. O Christ our God, who has appeared and enlightened the world, glory to you.*

Meeting Our Lord in the Temple

"A revealing light to the Gentiles, the glory of your people Israel" (Luke 2:32).

It is the person of Jesus Christ who brings God's love and glory into our lives. It is Jesus Christ who brings joy and light into our hearts.

The old man Simeon and the prophetess Anna are awaiting the fulfilment of God's promise of salvation. Simeon is so old that he can hardly see. But their faith is rewarded when Joseph and Mary bring Jesus to the Temple in Jerusalem, and Simeon exclaims: "My eyes have seen your saving deed!"

Jesus is the fulfilment of the Old Testament promises. He is the one who brings light and understanding to all. We follow him because he is our way, our salvation.

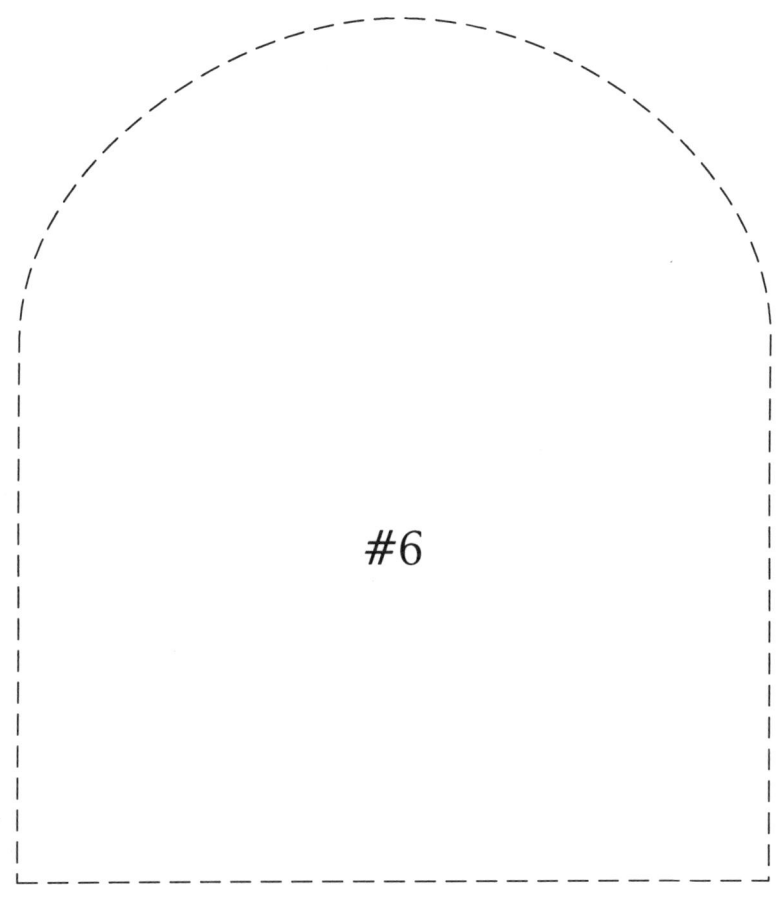

*Icon of the Presentation
of Our Lord Jesus Christ*

Tropar – *Hail, O virgin Mother of God, full of grace: for from you has shone forth the Sun of Righteousness, Christ our God, giving light to those in darkness. Be glad also, you righteous Elder, Simeon, for you have received in your arms the Deliverer of our souls, who bestows upon us Resurrection.*

The Entry into Jerusalem

"Rejoice and be glad, exalt and be most joyful . . . for behold your King has come in righteousness" (Vespers verse).

Jesus comes to us, and our hearts are truly filled with joy. Prayer is a serious activity, but it is also such a joyous event, because Christ comes into our hearts as he comes to Jerusalem on Palm Sunday. Everyone comes out to greet Jesus, but none shows such emotion, love and joy as the children who spread their cloaks along his way. They really love Jesus because they know he loves them.

So also in our prayer – once we recognize him, once we feel his presence, we don't hold back like the elders in Jerusalem, but let go and reach out to the Lord in joy.

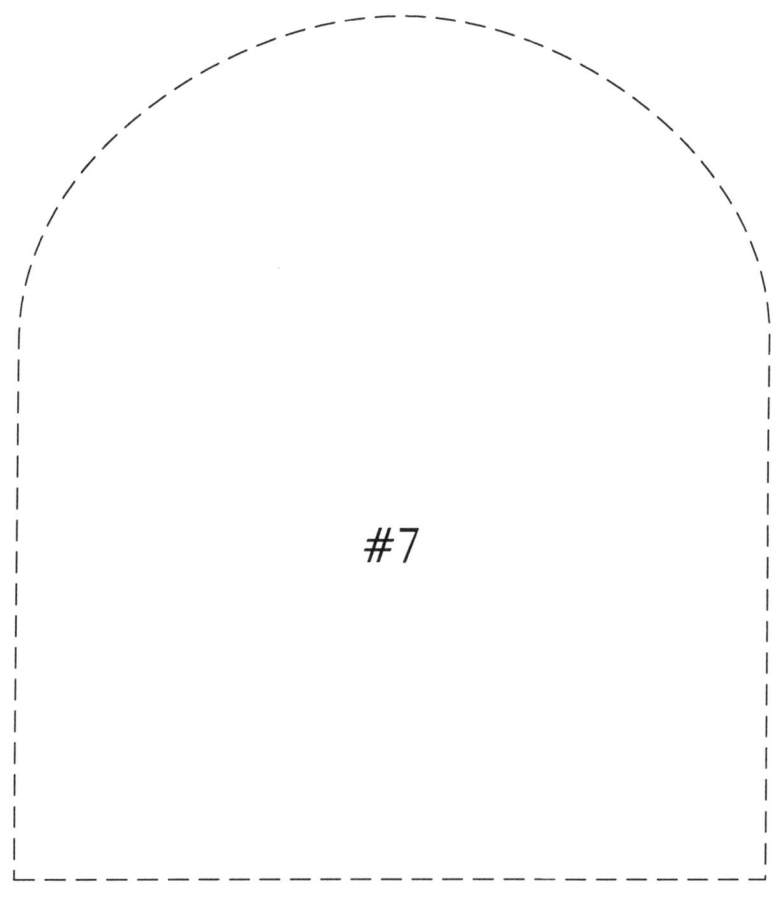

Icon of the Entry into Jerusalem

Tropar – *Giving us before your Passion an assurance of the general resurrection, you raised Lazarus from the dead, O Christ our God. Therefore, like children, we also carry tokens of victory, and cry to you, the Conqueror of Death: "Hosanna in the highest; blessed is he who comes in the name of the Lord."*

The Crucifixion of Our Lord

"I solemnly assure you, unless the grain of wheat falls to the earth and dies, it remains just a grain of wheat. But if it dies, it produces much fruit"
(John 12:24).

There is great joy in being a Christian, but to follow Jesus is also a difficult job. Jesus, the compassionate lover of humanity, was nailed to a Cross and allowed to die. To be a Christian is to follow him, even if that means being unpopular, being a loner, being outside the crowd. Christ lived as one of us, he suffered as one of us, and he died as one of us. There is no pain, no anxiety, no fear that we can experience that he has not also experienced. Jesus experienced true human life so that we will always know that he is with us.

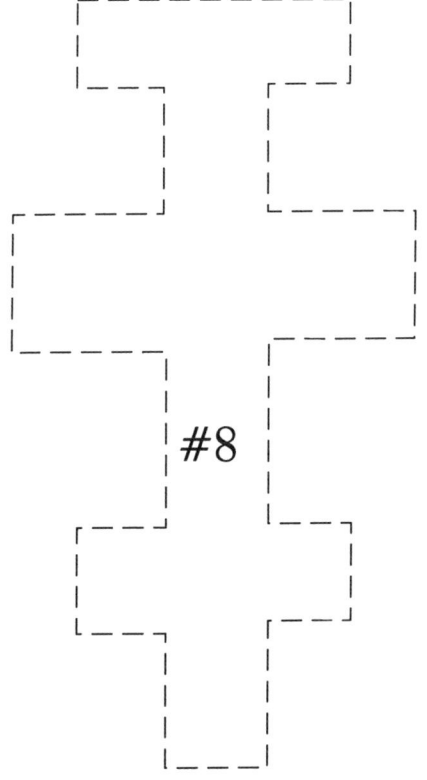

Icon of the Crucifixion of Christ

Antiphon Fifteen from Good Friday Matins –
Today he who hung the earth upon the waters is hung upon the Cross. He who is king of the angels is arrayed with a crown of thorns. He who wraps the heavens in clouds is wrapped in the purple of mockery.... We venerate your Passion, O Christ. Show us your glorious Resurrection.

The Resurrection of Our Lord

Victory is ours! Through the Cross comes Resurrection! Overcoming the pain, we can know true joy.

Jesus' death was not the last word; it was the first word – life everlasting. Jesus descended into the depths of the earth (Hades) and raised the righteous into new life. He raised Adam and Eve (who kneel before him), the Old Testament leaders – King David, Moses and Solomon (who stand behind him) – and everyone else who served God and waited for the coming of Christ.

The Resurrection shows us that nothing can truly separate us from God's love. God's love conquers everything! God's love never ends – not even with death!

Our prayer binds us to that love, to that everlasting life!

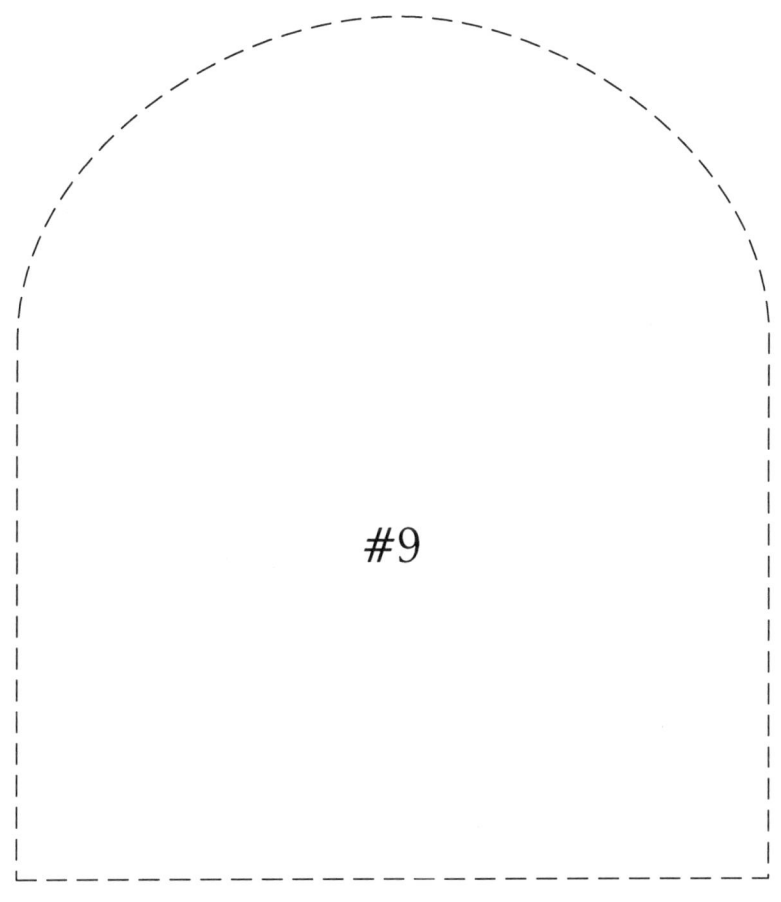

Icon of the Resurrection of Christ ("Descent into Hades")

Tropar – *Christ is risen from the dead, conquering death by death, and to those in the tombs, he granted life.*

The Ascension of Our Lord

"It is much better for you that I go" (John 16:7).

Christ ascends into Heaven forty days after his Resurrection, not because he doesn't want to be with us, but because we must receive the Holy Spirit. He does not leave us alone – he leaves us his community, his followers, his Church. In the icon we see the Mother of God surrounded by two groups of apostles. They represent the Church. Christ's words are remembered by them, and passed on by them. We never pray alone because they teach us how to pray. The Church prays with us. We all pray together.

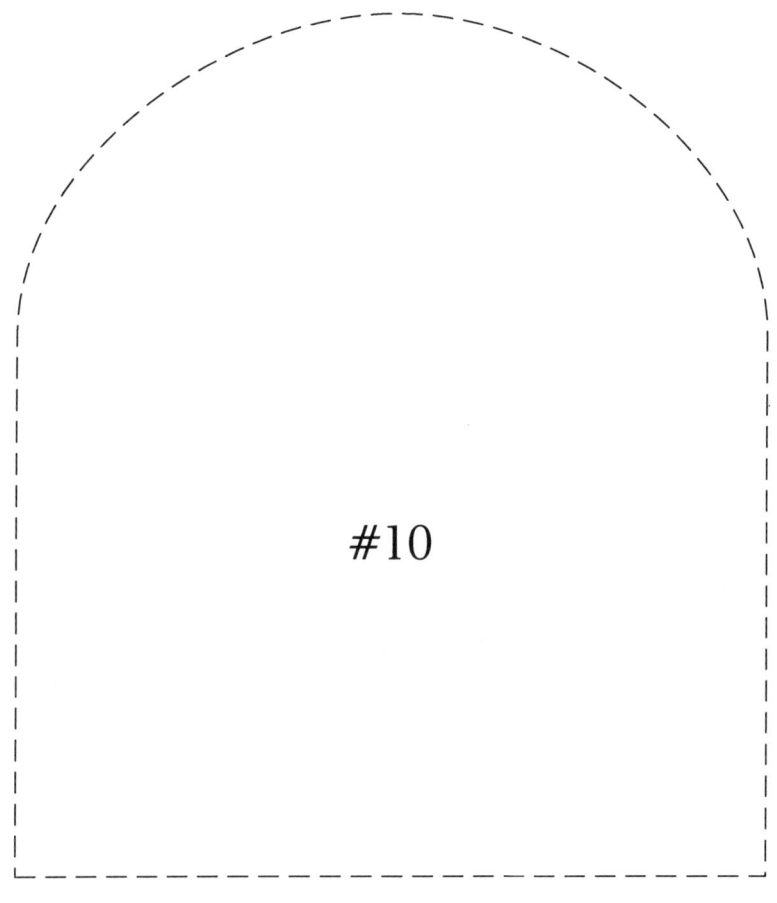

Icon of the Ascension of Our Lord

Tropar – *You ascended in glory, O Christ our God, and gladdened your disciples with the promise of the Holy Spirit. By your blessing they were assured that you are the Son of God, Saviour of the world.*

The Descent of the Holy Spirit

The Spirit comes to the community and through the community. The Spirit creates in us the bond of love which establishes the Church.

Mary, the Mother of the Church, holds her hands in prayer and leads the apostles in prayer. Many of the apostles are confused and perhaps even frightened by the descent of the Holy Spirit. But Mary is calm, prayerful and open, and her conduct comforts them and reminds them of her Son. She reminds them – and us – to pray.

There is an old man in the centre of the icon. Surrounded by Mary and the apostles, he symbolizes the world. He is there to remind us that we do not pray for ourselves alone, but for the entire world. The Holy Spirit descends on the apostles, and on us in Chrismation (Confirmation), so that we can carry the Spirit into the world. Our prayer helps to transform not only ourselves, but also our friends, our neighbours, our world.

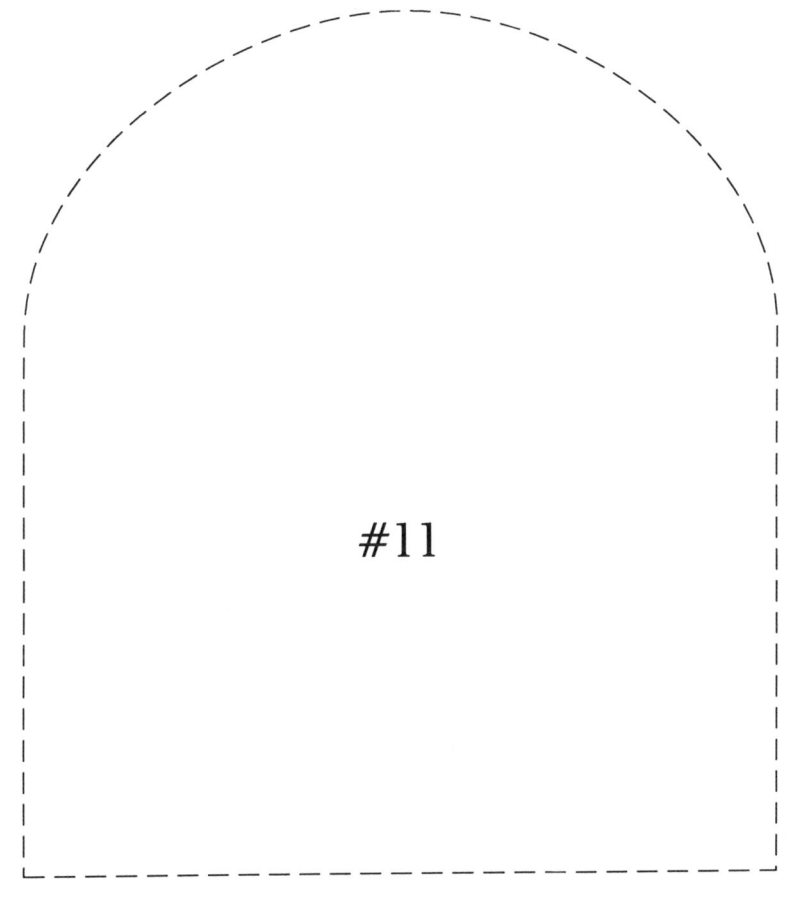

*Icon of the Descent of the Holy Spirit
– Pentecost*

Tropar – *Blessed are you, Christ our God, who made fishermen wise by sending the Holy Spirit down on them. You netted the world through them, loving Lord; glory to you.*

The Dormition of the Mother of God

The final feast of the liturgical year is the Dormition of the Mother of God. Dormition means "falling asleep." Mary falls asleep; she does not know the pain, anguish and fear of death because she is always united to the love of her Son, our Lord. Her passing is beautiful; she is the first saint. The Church, all the saints, gather around her. They are sad, but more than that, they are amazed as Jesus takes her to be with him in Eternity.

Mary's death is the death that we all hope for. She died as she lived – with Christ. She is the first saint, but we are all called by Jesus to be saints. We must get up, "go and do likewise," go and be icons of Christ in the world.

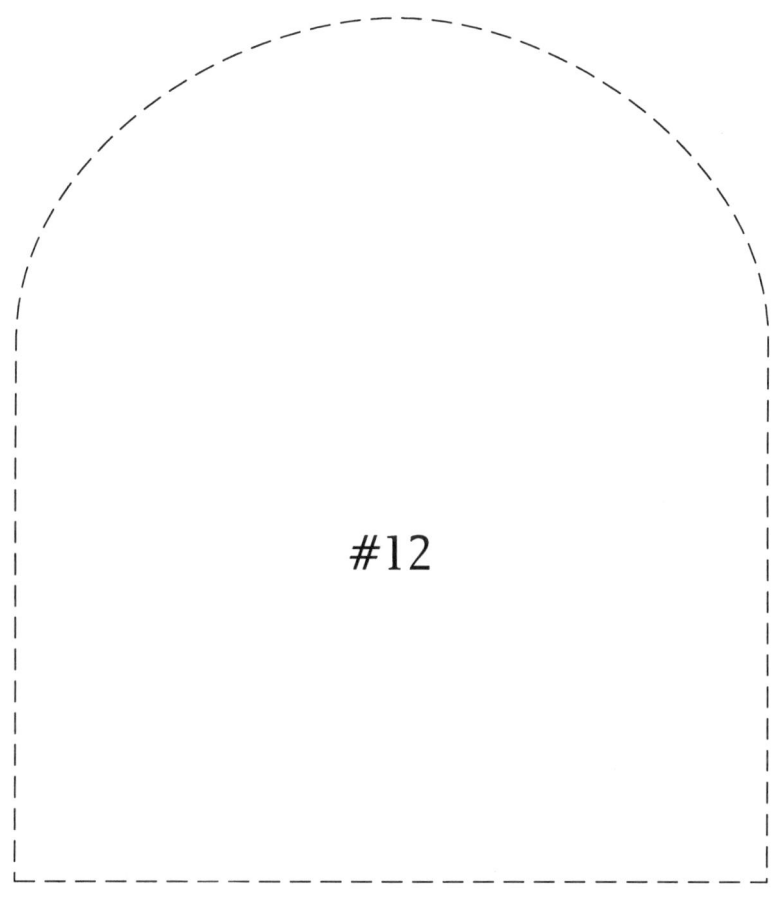

*Icon of the Dormition
of the Holy Mother of God*

Tropar – *In giving birth, O Mother of God, you retained your virginity, and in falling asleep you did not forsake the world. You who are the Mother of Life have passed over into life, and by your prayers you deliver our souls from death.*

Suggestions for Parents and Teachers

This little book was originally published as Praying with Icons: An Introduction for Children. *It soon became apparent, however, that people of all ages benefit from the approach taken here. This is an activity booklet designed to help readers be passive. But that is what prayer is about: doing things in the Lord, praying while we work. When your children or students want to pray with icons, let them take this booklet and go to it. Only ask that they do it slowly, carefully and joyfully.*

Once they have pasted the icons in the booklet, have them keep it somewhere special. Your home or classroom should have an icon corner where everyone can pray together or alone. Place the booklet in the corner and encourage the children to pray with it. Perhaps each child could complete his or her own personal copy of How To Pray with Icons. *On a given feast day you could then use it to pray together the appropriate* tropar *(the "proper," or special prayer of the feast). The children could even take turns sharing their reflections on the icon and the feast. Remember, icons are windows onto Heaven: the more we look into them, the more we pray with them, the closer we come to Heaven.*

God bless all of you in your efforts!